Rookie

Read-About® Math

Odd and Even Socks

By Melanie Chrismer

Consultant
Ari Ginsburg
Math Curriculum Specialist

Children's Press®
A Division of Scholastic Inc.
New York   Toronto   London   Auckland   Sydney
Mexico City   New Delhi   Hong Kong
Danbury, Connecticut

Designer: Herman Adler Design
Photo Researcher: Caroline Anderson
The photo on the cover shows a group of children wearing an even number of socks.

Library of Congress Cataloging-in-Publication Data

Chrismer, Melanie.
  Odd and even socks / by Melanie Chrismer.
    p. cm. — (Rookie read-about math)
  Includes index.
  ISBN 0-516-25265-8 (lib. bdg.)   0-516-25366-2 (pbk.)
  1. Numeration—Juvenile literature. 2. Numbers, Natural—Juvenile
literature. 3. Mathematics—Juvenile literature. I. Title. II. Series.
  QA141.3.C486 2005
  513.5—dc22   2005004617

CHILDREN'S PRESS, and ROOKIE READ-ABOUT®,
and associated logos are trademarks and/or registered trademarks
of Scholastic Library Publishing. SCHOLASTIC and associated logos
are trademarks and/or registered trademarks of Scholastic Inc.

1 2 3 4 5 6 7 8 9 10 R 14 13 12 11 10 09 08 07 06 05

Sorting socks is fun!

Sometimes one sock is left over.

That means there is an odd number of socks.

Odd numbers

Even numbers

There are two kinds
of numbers.

There are odd numbers
and even numbers.

All numbers are either
odd or even.

What makes a number
odd or even?

Even numbers can be split
into equal whole parts.

Odd numbers cannot.

One sock cannot be split into whole parts. One is odd.

Two socks are called a pair.
It takes two equal parts to
make a pair.

Split the pair apart, and you have two equal socks and none left over. Two is even.

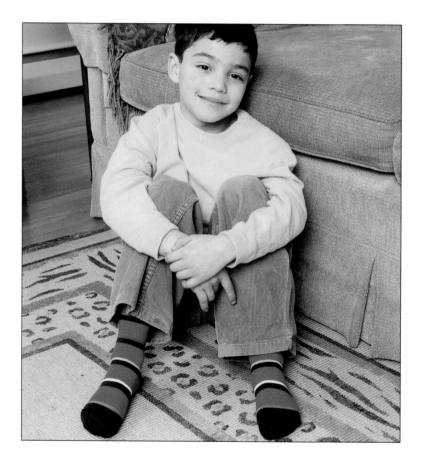

A number that can be split into equal parts with none left over is even.

A number that has one left over after you split it is odd.

Three socks can be split,
but a sock is left over.
Three is odd.

Four socks can be split
equally with none left
over. Four is even.

Five socks can be split,
but a sock is left over.
Five is odd.

Six socks can be split into two groups of three with none left over. Six is even.

Seven socks can be split,
but a sock is left over.
Seven is odd.

Eight socks can be split
with none left over. Eight
is even.

Nine socks can be split,
but a sock is left over.
Nine is odd.

Zero is different.

It does not follow the rule
for odd and even numbers.

If you have zero socks, you
cannot split them!

In a number line, every other number is odd or even.

Zero is found next to the number one.

One is odd. So zero is called an even number.

even odd even odd even odd even odd even odd

even   odd   even   odd   even   odd   even   odd   even odd

If you know the odd and even numbers from zero to nine, you know them all.

The digit that a number ends in tells you if that number is odd or even.

Five is odd. Fifteen and
any number that ends in
five is odd.

Eight is even. Twenty-eight and any number that ends in eight is even.

Zero is even.

One hundred and any number that ends in zero is even!

Words You Know

even   number line

odd

pair

socks

sorting

Index

About the Author

Melanie Chrismer is a writer and flutist who lives near Atlanta, Georgia. She loves reading, writing, and sorting socks without having any socks left over.

Photo Credits

All Photographs copyright © 2005 James Levin/Studio 10